Pebble™ Plus

Under the Sea

Sharks

by Carol K. Lindeen

Consulting Editor: Gail Saunders-Smith, PhD
Consultant: Jody Rake, Member
Southwest Marine/Aquatic Educator's Association

Capstone *press*

Mankato, Minnesota

Pebble Plus is published by Capstone Press
151 Good Counsel Drive, P.O. Box 669, Mankato, Minnesota 56002
www.capstonepress.com

1 2 3 4 5 6 09 08 07 06 05 04

Library of Congress Cataloging-in-Publication Data
Lindeen, Carol K., 1976–
    Sharks / by Carol K. Lindeen.
    p. cm.—(Pebble Plus: Under the sea)
    Includes bibliographical references (p. 23) and index.
    ISBN 0-7368-2602-5 (hardcover)
    1. Sharks—Juvenile literature. [1. Sharks.] I. Title. II. Series.
QL638.9.L54 2005
597.3—dc22   2003025612

Summary: Simple text and photographs present the lives of sharks.

Editorial Credits
Martha E. H. Rustad, editor; Juliette Peters, designer; Kelly Garvin, photo researcher;
    Karen Hieb, product planning editor

Photo Credits
Bruce Coleman Inc./Masa Ushioda/V&W, 16–17, 18–19
Corbis RF/Marty Snyderman, 1
Jeff Rotman, 6–7
Minden Pictures/Flip Nicklin, 13; Fred Bavendam, 4–5
PhotoDisc Inc., back cover
Seapics.com/Bob Cranston, 8–9; Doug Perrine, 14–15; James D. Watt, 20–21;
    Marilyn and Maris Kazmers, cover; Walt Stearns, 10–11

Note to Parents and Teachers

The Under the Sea series supports national science standards related to the diversity and
unity of life. This book describes and illustrates sharks. The images support early readers
in understanding the text. The repetition of words and phrases helps early readers learn
new words. This book also introduces early readers to subject-specific vocabulary words,
which are defined in the Glossary section. Early readers may need assistance to read
some words and to use the Table of Contents, Glossary, Read More, Internet Sites, and
Index/Word List sections of the book.

Word Count: 84
Early-Intervention Level: 13

Table of Contents

Sharks

What are sharks?
Sharks are fish.

Some sharks grow bigger
than a car. Other sharks
are the size of an
adult's hand.

Some sharks gather
in groups called schools.

9

Sharks have sharp
teeth. Sharks catch
fish and other animals
for food.

Sharks breathe through gills.

Gills are slits on the sides

of sharks.

Swimming

Sharks move their tails

from side to side

to swim.

Fins point out from

a shark's body.

Sharks use their fins
to swim, balance,
and steer.

Under the Sea

Sharks glide

under the sea.

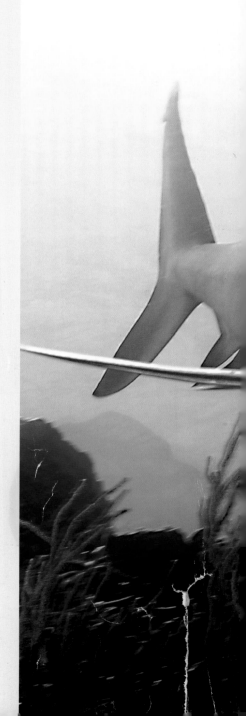

Glossary

balance—to keep steady and even; sharks use their fins to balance while swimming in the water.

fin—a thin body part on a swimming animal; sharks have five kinds of fins.

gill—a body part that a fish uses to breathe; gills are the slits on the sides of a shark's head.

glide—to move in a smooth and easy way

school—a group of fish; as many as one hundred hammerhead sharks may gather in a school.

steer—to move in a certain direction

Read More

Arnosky, Jim. *All about Sharks.* New York: Scholastic, 2003.

Baldwin, Carol. *Sharks.* Sea Creatures. Chicago: Heinemann Library, 2003.

Cole, Joanna. *Hungry, Hungry Sharks.* Step into Reading. New York: Random House, 2003.

Rustad, Martha E.H. *Sharks.* Ocean Life. Mankato, Minn.: Pebble Books, 2001.

Internet Sites

FactHound offers a safe, fun way to find Internet sites related to this book. All of the sites on FactHound have been researched by our staff.

Here's how:

1. Visit *www.facthound.com*

2. Type in this special code **0736826025** for age-appropriate sites. Or enter a search word related to this book for a more general search.

3. Click on the **Fetch It** button.

FactHound will fetch the best sites for you!

Index/Word List